WACO McLENNAN COUNTY L
1717 AUSTIN AVE.
WACO, TX 76701

MW01562439

Where in the World Can I...

MEET A GHOST?

Where in the World Can I... MEET A GHOST?

WORLD BOOK

www.worldbook.com

World Book, Inc.
180 North LaSalle Street, Suite 900
Chicago, Illinois 60601
USA

For information about other World Book publications, visit our website at **www.worldbook.com** or call **1-800-WORLDBK (967-5325).**

For information about sales to schools and libraries, call 1-800-975-3250 (United States), or 1-800-837-5365 (Canada).

© 2018 (print and e-book) by World Book, Inc. All rights reserved. No part of this publication may be reproduced, stored in a retrieval system, or transmitted in any form or by any means (electronic, mechanical, photocopying, recording, or otherwise) without written permission from World Book, Inc.

WORLD BOOK and the GLOBE DEVICE are registered trademarks or trademarks of World Book, Inc.

Library of Congress Cataloging-in-Publication Data for this volume has been applied for.

Where in the World Can I...
ISBN: 978-0-7166-2178-2 (set, hc.)

Meet a Ghost?
ISBN: 978-0-7166-2184-3 (hc.)

Also available as:
ISBN: 978-0-7166-2194-2 (e-book)

Printed in China by Shenzhen Wing King Tong Paper Products Co., Ltd., Shenzhen, Guangdong
1st printing July 2018

STAFF

Writer: Paul A. Kobasa

Executive Committee
President
 Jim O'Rourke

Vice President and Editor in Chief
 Paul A. Kobasa

Vice President, Finance
 Donald D. Keller

Vice President, Marketing
 Jean Lin

Vice President, International Sales
 Maksim Rutenberg

Vice President, Technology
 Jason Dole

Director, Human Resources
 Bev Ecker

Editorial
Director, New Print
 Tom Evans

Managing Editor, New Print
 Jeff De La Rosa

Senior Editor, New Print
 Shawn Brennan

Editor, New Print
 Grace Guibert

Librarian
 S. Thomas Richardson

Manager, Contracts & Compliance (Rights & Permissions)
 Loranne K. Shields

Manager, Indexing Services
 David Pofelski

Digital
Director, Digital Product Development
 Erika Meller

Manager, Digital Products
 Jonathan Wills

Graphics and Design
Senior Art Director
 Tom Evans

Coordinator, Design Development and Production
 Brenda Tropinski

Media Researcher
 Rosalia Bledsoe

Manufacturing/ Production
Manufacturing Manager
 Anne Fritzinger

Proofreader
 Nathalie Strassheim

TABLE OF CONTENTS

6	What Is a Ghost?
14	The Battle of Quebec—Source of Ghosts?
20	The Battle
26	Ghosts on the Plains of Abraham
30	Other "Haunted" Battlefields
	The Spanish Armada
	The Battle of Spotsylvania Court House
	The Battle of Passchendaele
44	Will You Meet a Ghost?
46	Books and Websites
47	Index
48	Acknowledgments

WHAT IS A GHOST?

A *ghost* is the spirit of a dead person that is in the living world. The *spirit* is the part of a living person that is not the person's body. A word that sometimes is used for spirit is *soul*. When a person dies, some people think that the person's spirit or ghost stays in the world or later comes back to the world.

There is no proof that there are ghosts. But from long ago until today, some people believe they have seen ghosts. The ghosts that people believe they have seen look like the living persons. But the ghosts seem to be shadows or are *transparent*—you can see through them.

Ghosts sometimes are shown as shapes covered in a white sheet. This probably is because the bodies of dead people may be wrapped in a cloth called a *shroud (shrowd)*. The ghost of the dead person comes back still wearing the person's shroud.

Empty old houses and other buildings and cemeteries are places where people think that ghosts can be. A *cemetery (SEHM uh tehr ee)* is a piece of land where the bodies of dead people are *buried*—put into the earth. Ghosts may be where sad or bad things happened. Ghosts seem mostly to be seen at night or in dark places.

Some ghosts seem to want to scare people. They may have done bad things as living people. Bad things may have happened to them.

"The Legend of Sleepy Hollow," by the American author Washington Irving, tells about a soldier who was killed in the American Revolution (1775-1783). His headless ghost rides a horse and scares people who pass the place where he died.

Other ghosts want to help people. The ghost of Jacob Marley is a character in Charles Dickens's book *A Christmas Carol*. Jacob's ghost visits his old partner in business, Ebenezer Scrooge, on a Christmas Eve in the 1800's. Jacob, helped by three other ghosts, shows Ebenezer how to be a better and happier person.

Some people are afraid of the ghosts of the dead. These people may say prayers or other special words to stop ghosts from coming back or to make them go away and stay away.

Other people try to bring the ghosts of the dead back. These people believe that ghosts can help them or keep them safe. They may put out things the person liked to eat or drink when the person was alive to invite the person's ghost back.

Some people believe that a person called a *medium* can talk to the ghosts of dead people. This belief is called *spiritualism (SPIHR uh chu uh LIHZ uhm)*. Spiritualists think that there is a connection between the physical world and the spiritual world. This connection does not end for a person when that person dies. The spirit reached by the medium may make sounds or move things to show that it is present. Some mediums may speak in the voice of the person who is dead.

THE BATTLE OF QUEBEC— SOURCE OF GHOSTS?

Quebec *(kwih BEHK,* or, in French, *kay BEHK)* is the capital city of the province of Quebec in eastern Canada. (In French, the name is spelled with an accent over the first *e, Québec.)* Quebec is the oldest city in Canada. The French explorer Samuel de Champlain set up a trading post along the St. Lawrence River in 1608. He called the trading post Quebec. Starting with only a few settlers then, more than 500,000 people live in the city now.

As you have read in the introduction, there seem to be more ghosts at places that are old. Quebec now is more than 400 years old. And some sad things have happened in Quebec. Ghosts also seem to gather where sad things happened. So, battlegrounds of long ago seem to be likely places to meet ghosts.

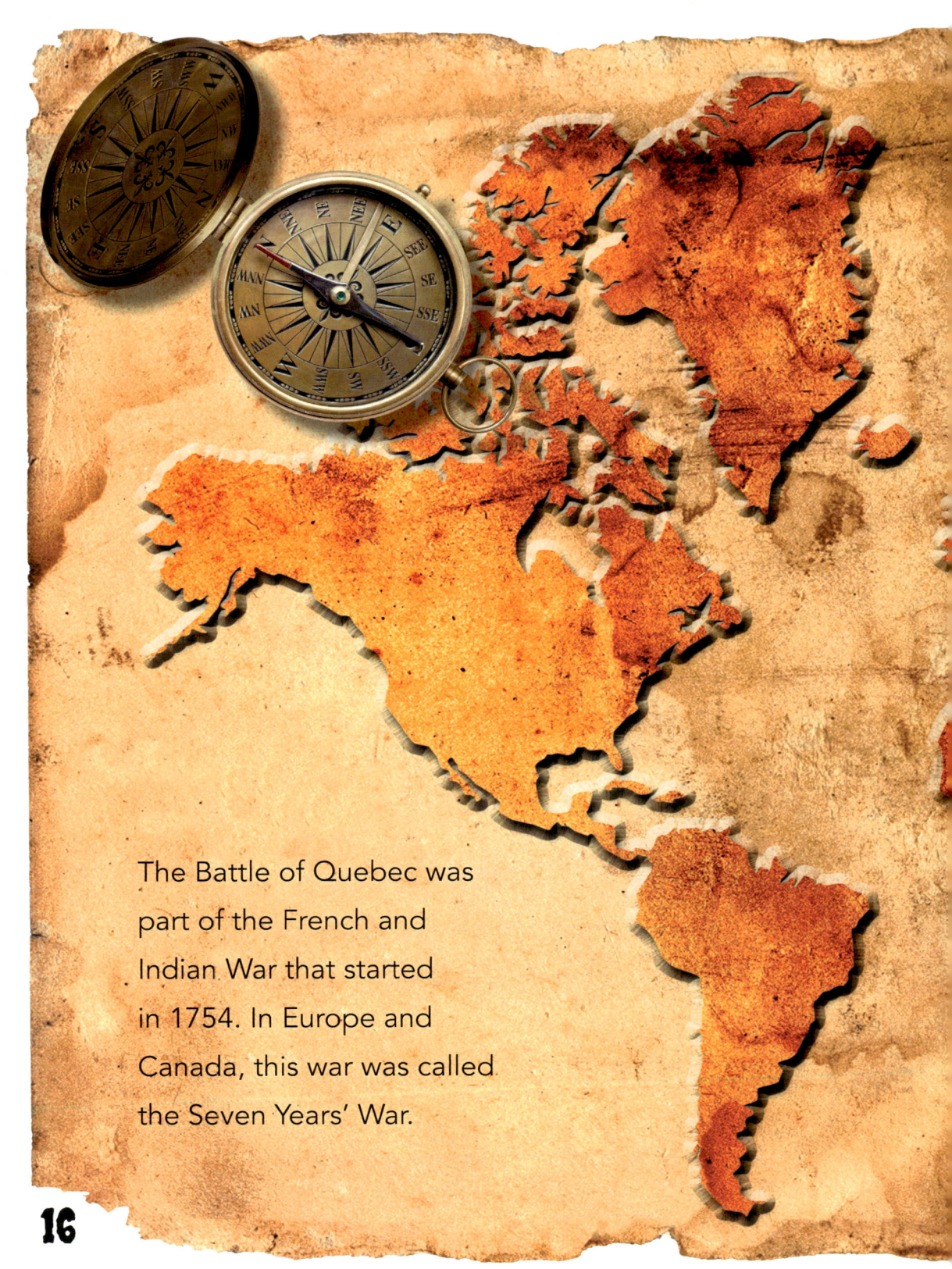

The Battle of Quebec was part of the French and Indian War that started in 1754. In Europe and Canada, this war was called the Seven Years' War.

In Europe, the armies of Prussia and Austria fought over control of territory. Britain was on Prussia's side. France was on Austria's side. Britain and France fought each other for control of the seas and land in North America.

There were four French and Indian wars. That is a lot of soldiers killed and a lot of sadness, making for the possibility of a lot of ghosts. The first of the wars, called King William's War, started in 1689. The Battle of Quebec was part of the last of the wars, the French and Indian War. This war started in 1754 and lasted until 1763.

The British and French rulers each wanted more land in North America. They went to war over land that both wanted. Some American Indians fought on the side of the French. Some fought on the side of the British. In Canada, American Indians are called First Nations peoples.

By 1759, Quebec was an important French city in North America. About 14,000 soldiers protected it. The Marquis *(mahr KEE)* of Montcalm was the commander of the French soldiers.

The year before, the British had taken over a French fort on an island in the Gulf of St. Lawrence. There, the British gathered a fleet of 250 ships to make an attack on Quebec. General James Wolfe was the leader. He had about 8,000 soldiers.

On the cloudy night of September 12-13, Wolfe's soldiers left their ships in small boats. The boats floated with the tide to a bay below the Plains of Abraham. In the night hours, about 4,500 British soldiers climbed a path up to the plains.

The Marquis of Montcalm thought the attack would happen in a different spot. He had to rush 4,000 of his soldiers to the Plains of Abraham to fight the invading British.

The shooting between the British and the French soldiers went on for only about 15 minutes. Many French soldiers were killed, and the British won the short battle. But British General Wolfe was killed by a French bullet.

The Marquis of Montcalm was wounded in the battle. He died in Quebec the next day. A few days later, on September 18, the city was handed over to British General George Townshend.

AND NOW FOR THE GHOSTS!

GHOSTS ON THE PLAINS OF ABRAHAM

Today the Plains of Abraham is the National Battlefields Park in Quebec City. The area probably was named for Abraham Martin. Martin was born in France in 1589. He died in Quebec in 1664. Between 1635 and 1645, he was given 32 acres (about 13 hectares) of land on a high area above the St. Lawrence River.

Many events in the history of Quebec, including the battle in 1759, happened on the Plains of Abraham. The area was made a park in 1908 as a memorial of that battle (and another battle in 1760). The park now is a beautiful green space in the middle of the big and busy city.

Some people who have visited the National Battlefields Park say they have seen shadowy figures there. These figures are dressed in the uniforms of soldiers of the 1700's. Along with these figures, there are the echoes of musket *(MUHS kiht)* fire. (A *musket* is a type of gun.) Some people believe they hear the cries of dying soldiers.

Do the ghosts of Wolfe and Montcalm come back to fight the battle again and again? Or the ghosts of the more than 100 French soldiers killed in the battle? Almost 60 British soldiers were killed. Their ghosts may haunt the plains, too.

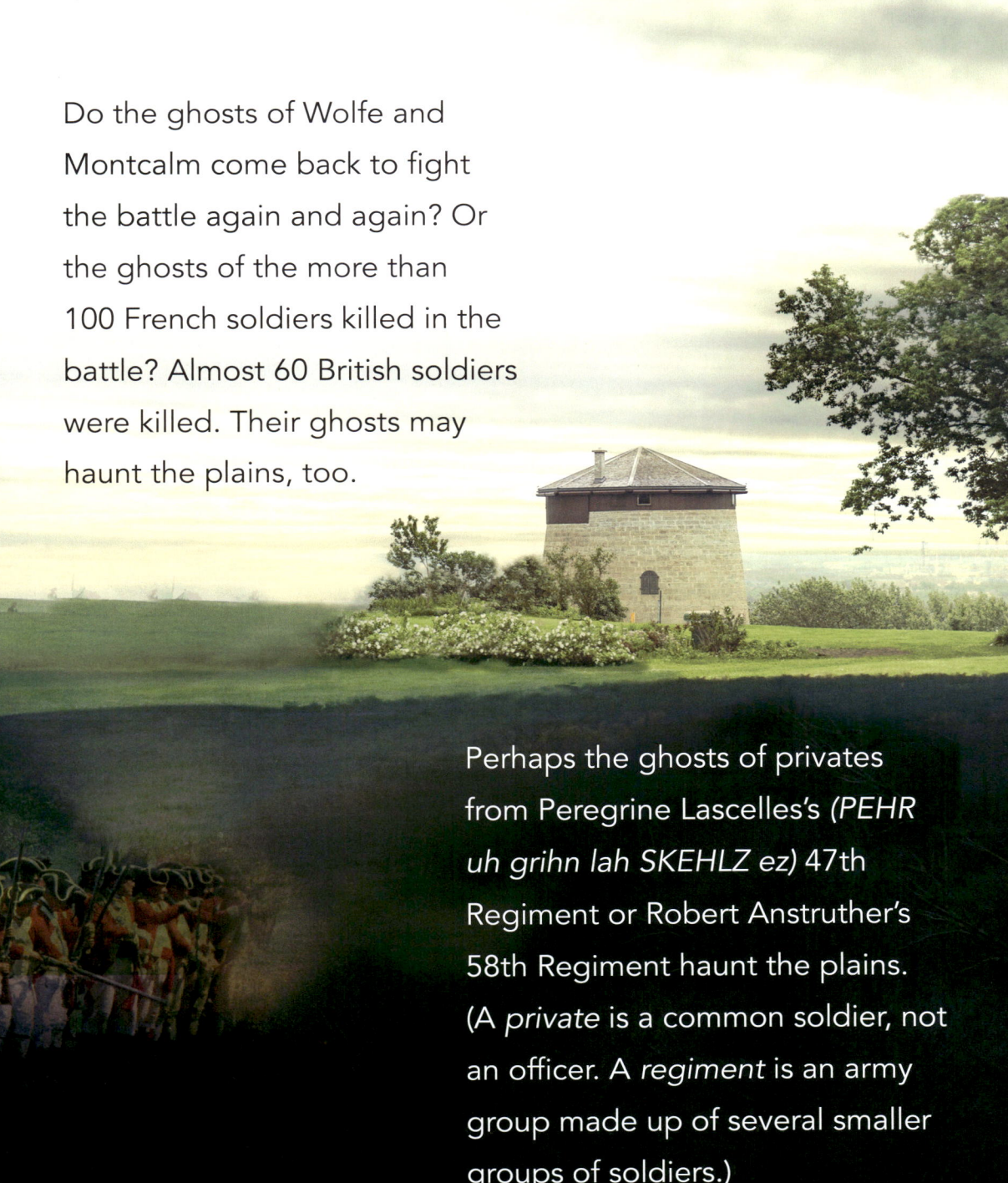

Perhaps the ghosts of privates from Peregrine Lascelles's *(PEHR uh grihn lah SKEHLZ ez)* 47th Regiment or Robert Anstruther's 58th Regiment haunt the plains. (A *private* is a common soldier, not an officer. A *regiment* is an army group made up of several smaller groups of soldiers.)

Other "Haunted" Battlefields

The Spanish Armada

The sea may be home to just as many ghosts as seem to be on dry land. There have been terrible battles at sea like there have been on land. One of the most historic of these battles was fought by warships of England and Spain in 1588.

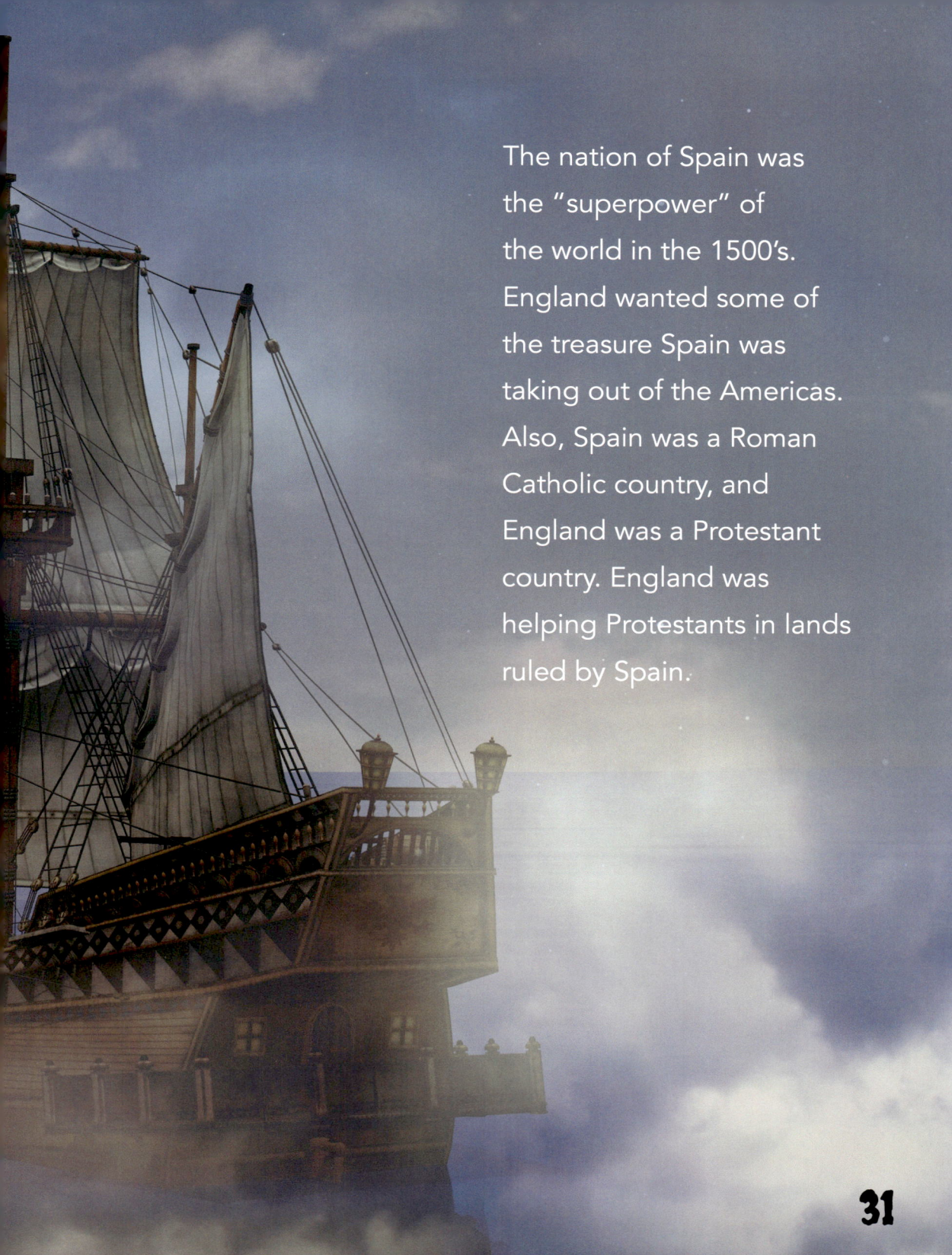

The nation of Spain was the "superpower" of the world in the 1500's. England wanted some of the treasure Spain was taking out of the Americas. Also, Spain was a Roman Catholic country, and England was a Protestant country. England was helping Protestants in lands ruled by Spain.

King Philip II of Spain decided to build a fleet of ships to carry soldiers to invade England. He called this fleet of ships the Armada. (In English, *armada [ahr MAH duh]* means a large group of military vehicles, in this case, warships.) There were 130 ships in the Armada. More than 29,000 soldiers and sailors sailed on the ships.

The Armada arrived in the English Channel at the end of July 1588. The English sent fire ships out among the Spanish ships. (A *fire ship* is filled with explosives, set on fire, and sent toward enemy ships.)

The Spanish ships headed out to sea. A fleet of smaller English ships attacked the Spanish ships.

The Spanish ships left after the attack sailed into the North Sea around the islands of Great Britain and Ireland. Many of these ships were wrecked in storms along Ireland's coast. As many as 5,000 Spanish sailors drowned or were captured and executed by the British.

Wrecks of some of the Spanish ships have been discovered on the ocean floor close to the coast of Ireland. Gold and silver Spanish coins and rings and other pieces of jewelry have been recovered. Some say the ghosts of the owners of these things cry out when the objects are taken to the surface.

The Battle of Spotsylvania Court House

The American Civil War tragically divided the United States from April 1861 until April 1865. This war took more American lives than any other war in history. The war was between the government of the United States and a group of states that left the union. These states formed the Confederate States of America.

The U.S. government wanted to maintain the union of all states. The main disagreement between the government and the Confederacy was slavery.

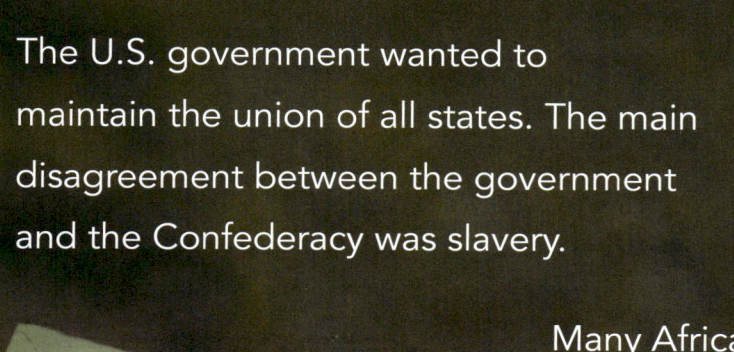

Many African American slaves were owned by farmers and others in the Confederacy. These slaveowners were afraid the government would end slavery.

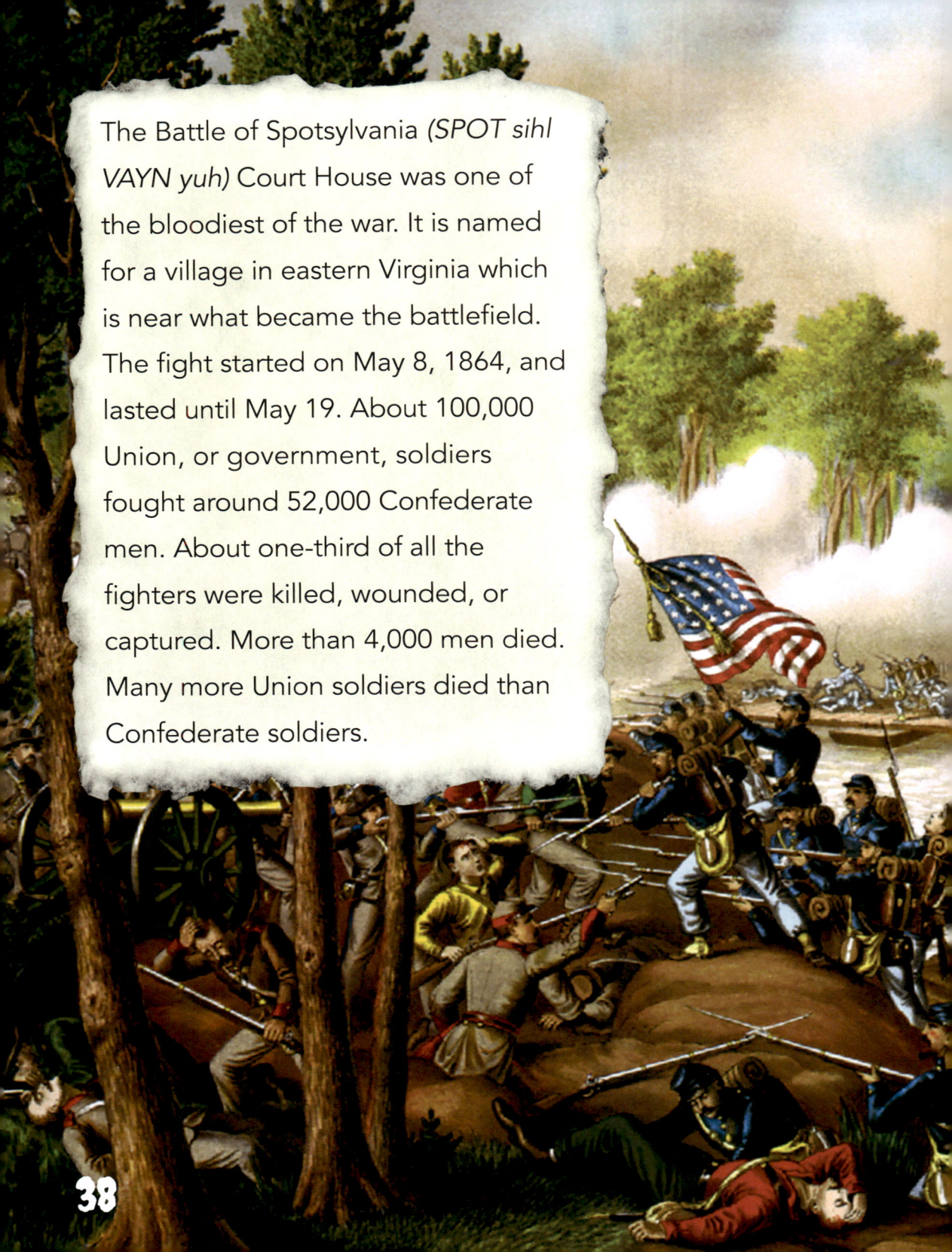

The Battle of Spotsylvania (SPOT sihl VAYN yuh) Court House was one of the bloodiest of the war. It is named for a village in eastern Virginia which is near what became the battlefield. The fight started on May 8, 1864, and lasted until May 19. About 100,000 Union, or government, soldiers fought around 52,000 Confederate men. About one-third of all the fighters were killed, wounded, or captured. More than 4,000 men died. Many more Union soldiers died than Confederate soldiers.

Some visitors to the battlefield say that they have heard cannon and musket fire. Others say that they have seen the shapes of figures—some running, some falling as if shot. These things seem to happen mostly at the spot called the "Bloody Angle." This is where some of the worst fighting of the battle took place.

Union Army Major General John Sedgwick and brigadier generals James Clay Rice and Thomas Stevenson died on the field or from wounds they received in the battle. On the Confederate side, brigadier generals Junius Daniel and Abner Monroe Perrin died. Maybe their ghosts are some of those haunting this place.

THE BATTLE OF PASSCHENDAELE

First known as the Great War, what today is called World War I started in 1914 and ended in 1918. About 9 million troops died, and more than 6 million regular citizens were killed. Two groups of nations fought in the war. One group was called the Allies, and the other group was called the Central Powers.

Three World War I battles took place near the city of Ypres *(EE pruh)* in the northwest corner of the country of Belgium.

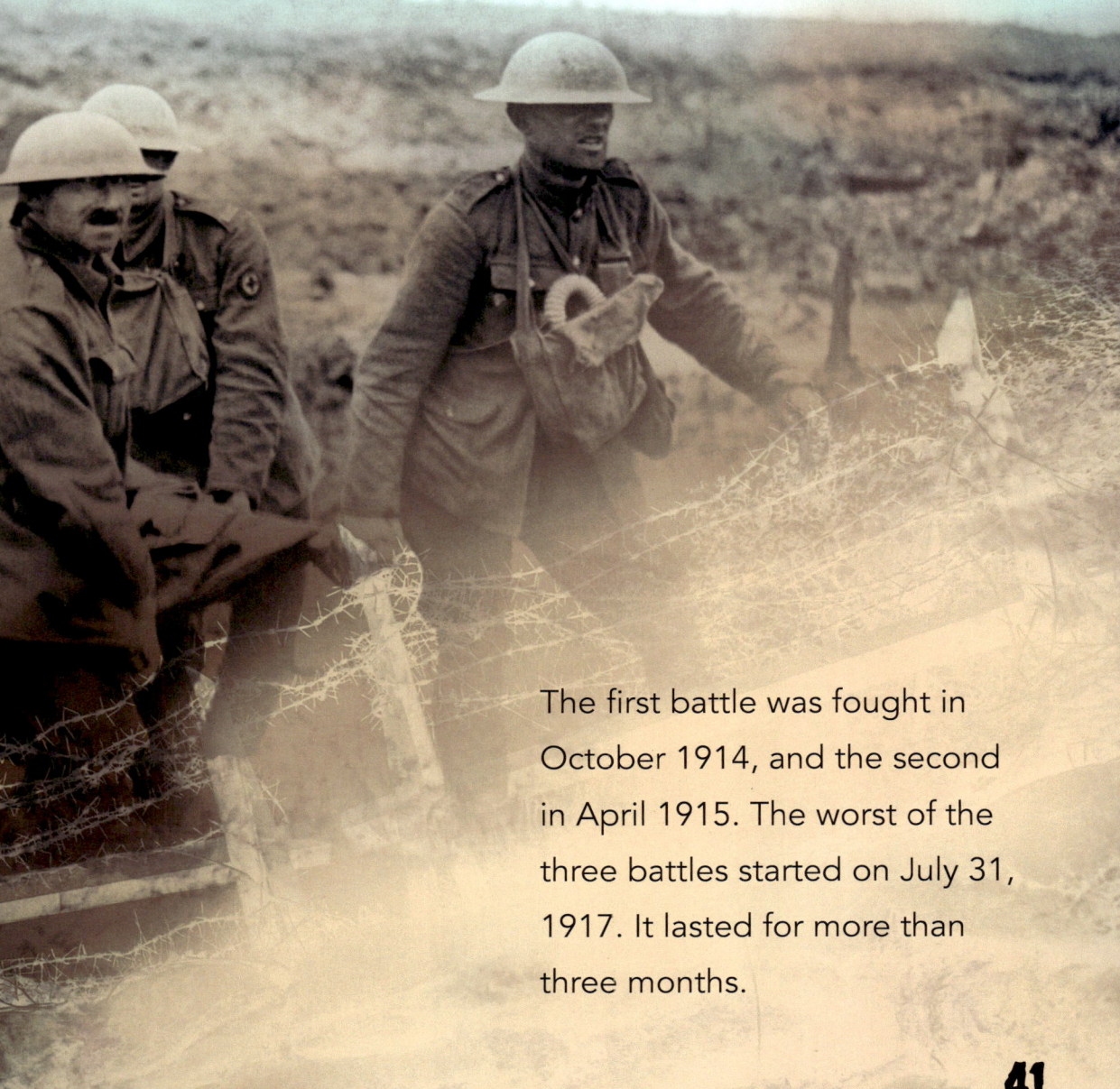

The first battle was fought in October 1914, and the second in April 1915. The worst of the three battles started on July 31, 1917. It lasted for more than three months.

The third battle of Ypres is called the Battle of Passchendaele (PASH uhn dayl). The battle was named for the village, close to Ypres, where it was fought. There were more than 250,000 Allied casualties. Germany, one of the Central Powers, had 200,000 casualties. (A *casualty* is a soldier, sailor, or other member of the armed forces who has been wounded, killed, captured, or has fallen ill as a result of enemy action.)

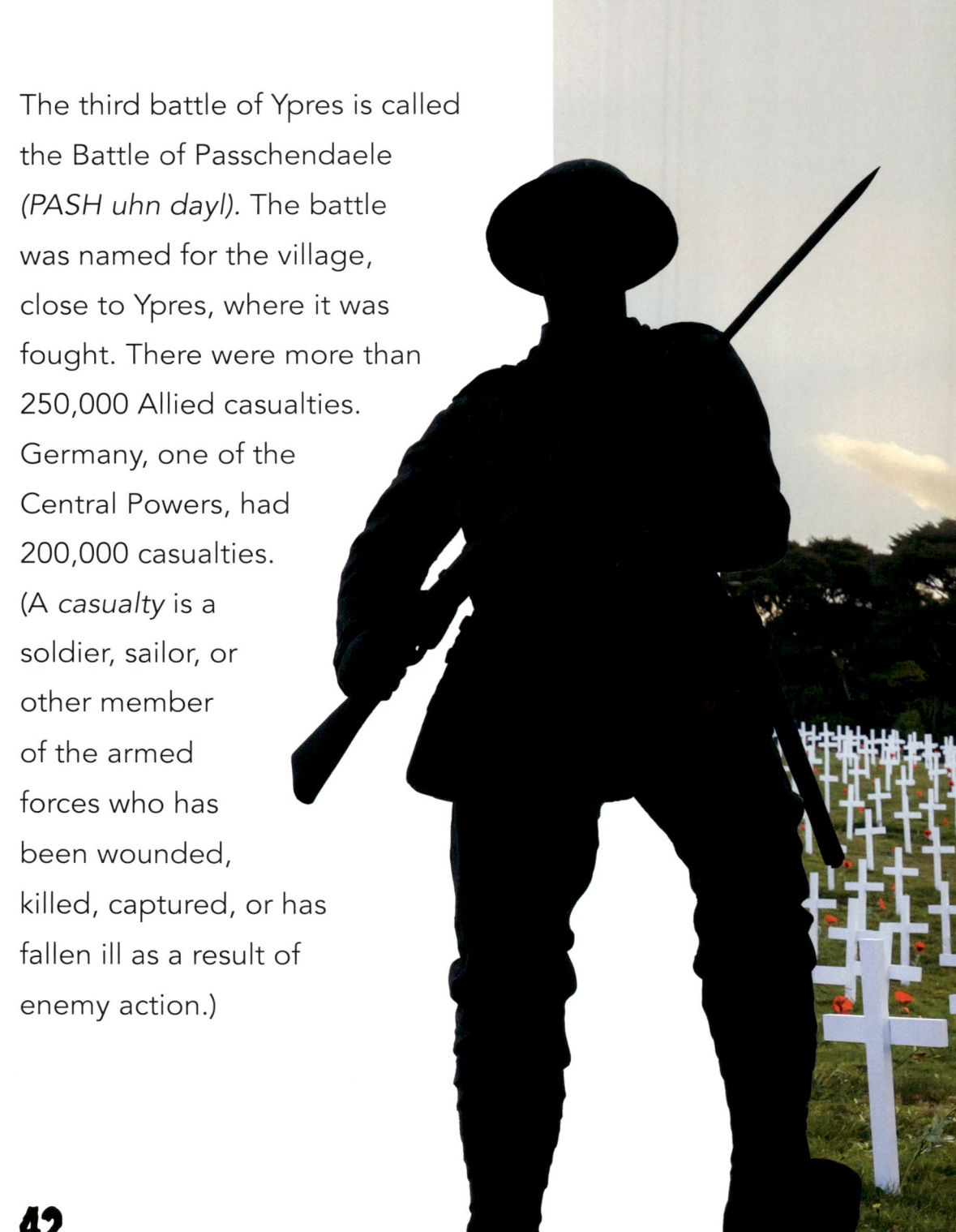

Soldiers from Australia, Britain, Canada, New Zealand, and South Africa fought against the German soldiers. The village fields were horribly torn up by heavy shelling. Heavy rains turned the fields into lakes of mud. Many of the dead never were found. Some people say they have heard the screams of the dying and smelled the smoke of battle in the countryside around the village.

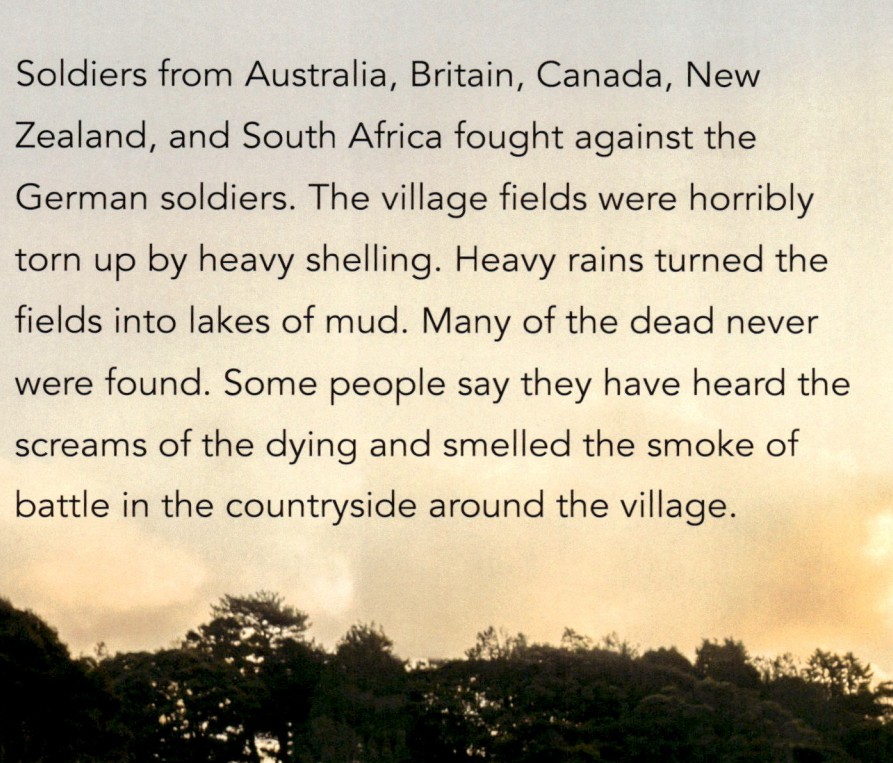

WILL YOU MEET A GHOST?

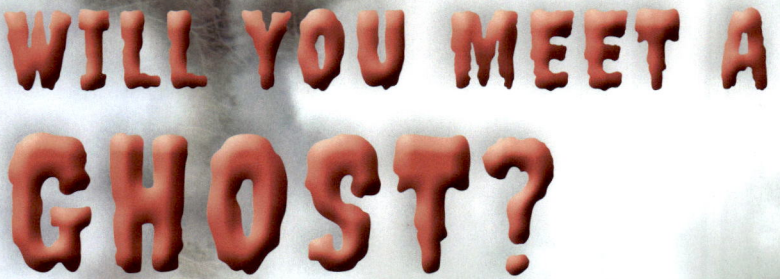

You might hike along the rocky edge of Lacada Point in County Antrim of Northern Island where one of the Spanish Armada warships was wrecked. Or you might look out over the Plains of Abraham or the fields of Spotsylvania or Passchendaele…and you might hear a sad sigh or catch the smell of gunpowder.

A sorrowful sailor of the Armada? A French farmer made to fight in Quebec? A New Englander killed by a Confederate sharpshooter? An Australian whose body was never found where it fell dead at Passchendaele?

You might not meet a ghost at any of these places or any other place either. But at these places of war, reflect with respect upon those who died there. Think about the terrible cost of war in human lives. Find out more about the history of these places and their battles. Your thoughts might help a weary ghost finally find peace.

BOOKS AND WEBSITES

BOOKS

Biggest, Baddest Book of Ghosts by Aaron DeYoe (ABDO, 2015)
This full-color, magazine-style book for kids explains some common types of ghosts and describes a few famously haunted places.

Cursed Grounds by Steven L. Stern (Bearport, 2011)
Each two-page spread focuses on a single horrifying habitat and is illustrated with photographs and period illustrations. Includes fun facts, a map, and glossary.

Ghosts by John Malam (Black Rabbit/QEB, 2010)
This book alternates "scary stories" (most of them allegedly true) with basic facts on detecting and dispatching ghosts. Includes timelines on pop-culture and other landmarks.

WEBSITES

Kids.Ghostvillage.com
http://kids.ghostvillage.com/
A resource for kids, parents, and educators who want some help in framing the discussion of the supernatural with a younger audience.

Battlefield of Spotsyvania Court House
https://www.civilwar.org/learn/civil-war/battles/spotsylvania-court-house

This site from the Civil War Trust contains histories, battlefield maps, videos and animations, biographies, photos, illustrations, and preservation news.

In Flanders Fields Museum
http://www.inflandersfields.be/

Ypres war museum website.

National Battlefield Commission - Plains of Abraham
http://www.ccbn-nbc.gc.ca/en/

Official website of the Plains of Abraham National Battlefields Commission. Includes historical information, an interactive Internet exhibit on the battle, videos, photos, illustrations, and resources.

INDEX

Abraham, Martin, 26
Abraham, Plains of, 22–23, 26–29, 44
Allies, 40, 42
American Indians, 19
American Revolution, 11
Anstruther, Robert, 29

battlegrounds, and ghosts, 15, 44–45
Bloody Angle, 39
British, 17–25, 29-34

cemeteries, 9
Central Powers, 40, 42
Champlain, Samuel de, 14
Christmas Carol, A, 11
Civil War, American, 36–39
Confederacy, 36–39

Daniel, Junius, 39
Dickens, Charles, 11

England, 30–34

fire ships, 33
France, 17–25
French and Indian War, 16, 18

ghosts, 6–13, 44–45
    of Passchendaele battle, 43-45
    of Quebec battle, 28–29, 45
    of Spanish Armada, 34–35, 44, 45
    of Spotsylvania Court House battle, 39, 44

Ireland, 34, 35
Irving, Washington, 11

Lascelles, Peregrine, 29
"Legend of Sleepy Hollow, The," 10–11

mediums, 13
Montcalm, Marquis of, 21, 23, 25, 29
muskets, 28, 39

National Battlefields Park, 26–29

Passchendaele, Battle of, 40–45
Perrin, Abner Monroe, 39
Philip II, King, 32

Quebec, Battle of, 14–19, 45

Rice, James Clay, 39

Sedgwick, John, 39
shrouds, 8
slavery, 37
souls, 6
Spain. *See* Spanish Armada
Spanish Armada, 30–35, 44, 45
spirits, 6
spiritualism, 13
Spotsylvania Court House, Battle of the, 36–39, 44, 45
Stevenson, Thomas, 39

Union soldiers, 38, 39

Wolfe, James, 21, 22, 24, 29
World War I, 40–43

Ypres, battles of, 41–43

ACKNOWLEDGMENTS

Cover: © Johnny Greig, iStockphoto; © Oonal/iStockphoto; © Lario Tus, Shutterstock; © Franciscah/Dreamstime

2-3 Public Domain

5-7 © Shutterstock

8-9 © legna69/iStockphoto; © Shutterstock

10-11 Fred Norris, FOX; © LightField Studios/Shutterstock; National General Pictures

12-13 © Shutterstock

14-15 © Shutterstock; © Jeff Greenberg, Getty Images

16-17 © Shutterstock

18-19 © Inspired By Maps/Shutterstock; © Vladvitek/Dreamstime

20-21 © TA Photography/Shutterstock; © Paul J. Richards, Getty Images

22-23 *View of the capture of Québec, September 13, 1759* (1787), Engraving on steel with heightenings in watercolor; Library and Archives Canada; © Evgenii Bobrov, Shutterstock

24-25 *The Battle of Sainte-Foy* (circa 1850's), watercolor with pencil by George Bryant Campion; Library and Archives Canada; *The Death of General Wolfe* (1857), engraving by Alonzo Chappel; Library and Archives Canada; © Bettmann/Getty Images

26-27 © laughingmango/iStockphoto; © Shutterstock

28-29 © Shutterstock; © Eitan Simanor, Alamy Images

30-31 © Shutterstock

32-33 *Defeat of the Spanish Armada, 8 August 1588* (1796), oil on canvas by Philip James de Loutherbourg; National Maritime Museum

34-35 © Shutterstock; National Maritime Museum

36-37 © Shutterstock

38-39 Library of Congress; © Fekete Tibor, Shutterstock

40-41 Imperial War Museum; © MSK Photography/Shutterstock

42-45 © Shutterstock